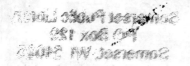

today and today

haiku by Kobayashi Issa

pictures by G. Brian Karas

scholastic press

new york

a word from the artist

Issa, a well-loved poet of haiku, was born Kobayashi Yataro in Japan in 1763. His life was not an easy or happy one. Though he was poor, he saw the riches in everyday life and the beauty of everyday moments. He was able to share his deepest feelings in his poetry.

Haiku tries to capture a single moment, like a snapshot of time or a feeling, in a way that reveals the beauty of that moment and what it tells us about life. Haiku poems traditionally use images from the natural world and are set in a particular season. The season may be named directly or hinted at through an image of nature. A cherry blossom, for instance, would show that the poem is set in spring. Traditional haiku also have a very structured form—three lines of five, seven, and five syllables. When translated into other languages, the syllable structure is sometimes lost, but the essential spirit of the poems remains.

Issa wrote his poems from deep within his own heart, and they express feelings that we all share. And so they seem to speak to everyone personally. Each of Issa's poems tell of a moment in his life, but for this book I have chosen and arranged eighteen of his haiku to tell the story of a year in the life of an imaginary family. They are not Issa's family, or my family, or yours. But the moments they experience—big and small, private and shared, happy and sad—are all moments in the cycle of life.

In my artwork, I have tried to achieve visually what Issa achieves with words, to convey the precise feeling of each moment so that someone else might feel it, too. The buzz of a hot summer day or big wet snowflakes hitting your face—it is ordinary, extraordinary moments like these, strung together, that make up our lives.

for my family

with special thanks to David Saylor, who thought I should illustrate a book of haiku

and thank you to Liz Szabla and Lauren Thompson for all the right words —G. B. K.

All rights reserved. Published by Scholastic Press, an imprint of Scholastic Inc., *Publishers since 1920.* SCHOLASTIC, SCHOLASTIC PRESS, and associated logos are trademarks and/or registered trademarks of Scholastic Inc.

Library of Congress Cataloging-in-Publication Data
Kobayashi, Issa, 1763-1827. [Poems. English. Selections] Today and today / by Issa ; selected and illustrated by G. Brian Karas.   p. cm.   1. Kobayashi, Issa, 1763-1827—Translations into English. 2. Haiku—Translations into English. I. Karas, G. Brian. II. Title.   PL797.2 . A247 2007   895.6'13—dc22   2003026684
ISBN-13: 978-0-439-59078-5   ISBN-10: 0-439-59078-7

Printed in Singapore 46   10 9 8 7 6 5 4 3 2 1   07 08 09 10 11
First edition, March 2007
The text type was set in Neutra Text Book.
Book design by David Saylor and Charles Kreloff

"Once snows have melted," "Just being alive!," "Today and today," "In hazy spring mist," "So many breezes," "How well we have slept," "The field wren," "The first snow has fallen," "Calm, indifferent," and "As simple as that—" from *The Spring of My Life: and Selected Haiku* by Kobayashi Issa, translated by Sam Hamill. Copyright © 1997 by Sam Hamill. Reprinted by arrangement with Shambhala Publications, Inc., Boston, www.shambhala.com. • "The spring day," "With my father," "Summer night—," "Autumn moon—," and "Here" from *The Essential Haiku: Versions of Basho, Buson, and Issa*, edited and with an Introduction by Robert Hass. Introduction and selection copyright © 1994 by Robert Hass. Unless otherwise noted, all translations copyright © 1994 by Robert Hass. Reprinted by permission of HarperCollins Publishers Ltd. • "It begins" from *inch by inch: 45 Haiku by Issa*, translated by Nanao Sakaki. Translation copyright © 1999 by Nanao Sakaki. Reprinted by permission of La Alameda Press.

spring

Once snows have melted,
the village soon overflows
with friendly children

Just being alive!
—miraculous to be in
cherry blossom shadows!

Today and today
also—a kite entangled
in a gnarled tree

In hazy spring mist,
sitting inside the great hall,
not a hint of sound

The spring day
lingers
in the pools

summer

With my father
I would watch dawn
over green fields

It begins

from the cicada's song

the gentle breeze

So many breezes
wander through my summer room:
but never enough

Summer night—

even the stars

are whispering to each other

autumn

How well we have slept
to feel so fresh this morning,
dear chrysanthemums!

Autumn moon—
a small boat
drifting down the tide

winter

The first snow has fallen
and now lies alone and white
out behind our house

The field wren,
searching here, there, everywhere—
has she lost something?

Calm, indifferent
as if nothing's transpired—
the goose, the willow

Here
I'm here—
the snow falling

As simple as that—
spring has finally arrived
with a pale blue sky

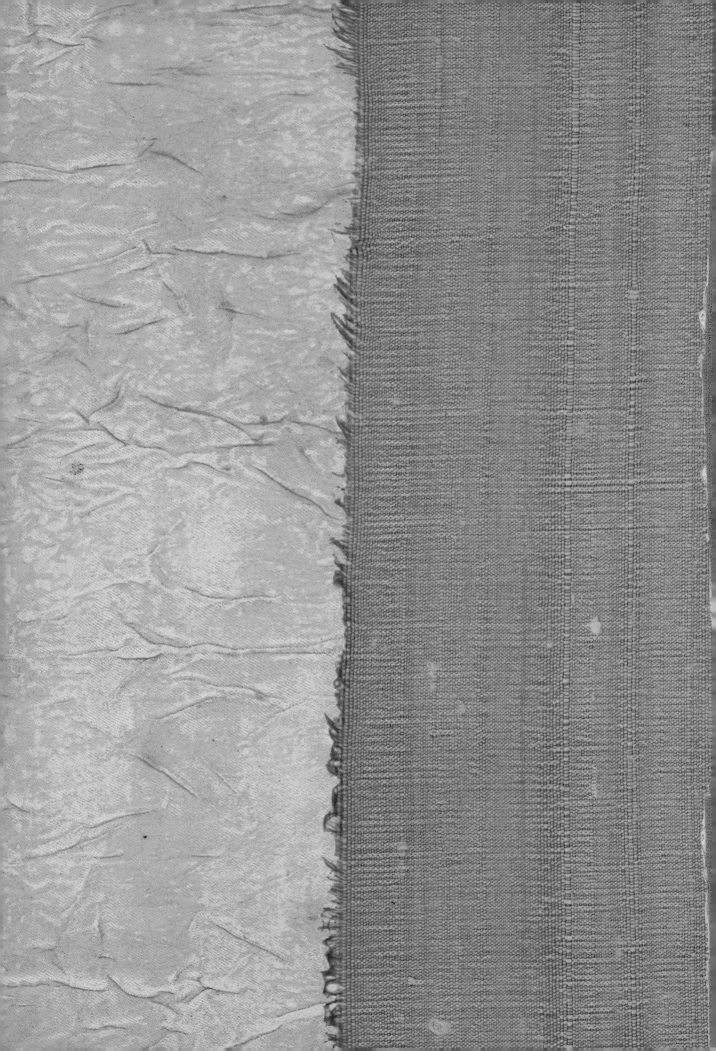